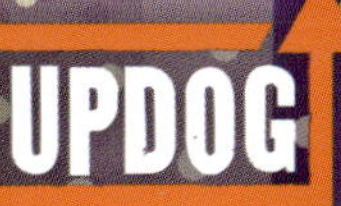

IN THE SPOTLIGHT

MrBEAST

RECORD-BREAKING YOUTUBER

Rachel Rose

Lerner Publications ◆ Minneapolis

Lerner Publications Company
An imprint of Lerner Publishing Group, Inc.
241 First Avenue North
Minneapolis, MN 55401 USA

For reading levels and more information, look up this title at www.lernerbooks.com.

Main body text set in ITC Franklin Gothic Std.
Typeface provided by Adobe Systems.

Editor: Angel Kidd **Designer:** Martha Kranes **Photo Editor:** Angel Kidd

Library of Congress Cataloging-in-Publication Data

Names: Rose, Rachel, 1968– author.
Title: MrBeast : record-breaking YouTuber / Rachel Rose.
Description: Minneapolis : Lerner Publications, [2026] | Series: Updog books. In the spotlight | Includes bibliographical references and index. | Audience: Ages 8–11 | Audience: Grades 2–3 | Summary: "MrBeast is the largest YouTube channel in the world and continues to grow exponentially. Readers will love learning all about Jimmy Donaldson, from his jaw-dropping challenge videos to his heartwarming philanthropy work"— Provided by publisher.
Identifiers: LCCN 2024037258 (print) | LCCN 2024037259 (ebook) | ISBN 9798765669204 (lib. bdg.) | ISBN 9798765684511 (pbk.) | ISBN 9798765679173 (epub)
Subjects: LCSH: MrBeast, 1998– —Juvenile literature. | Bloggers—United States—Biography—Juvenile literature. | Internet personalities—United States—Biography—Juvenile literature. | Video blogs—United States—Juvenile literature. | YouTube (Firm)—Biography—Juvenile literature.
Classification: LCC PN1992.9236.M73 R67 2026 (print) | LCC PN1992.9236.M73 (ebook) | DDC 302.23/14092 [B]—dc23/eng/20241010

LC ebook record available at https://lccn.loc.gov/2024037259

Manufactured in the United States of America
1-1011540-53891-10/31/2024

TABLE OF CONTENTS

Starting Young

MrBeast grinned as the crowd cheered.

He had won the 2023 Kids' Choice Award for Favorite Male Creator.

MrBeast's real name is Jimmy Donaldson.

Jimmy was thirteen when he started his first YouTube channel in 2012.

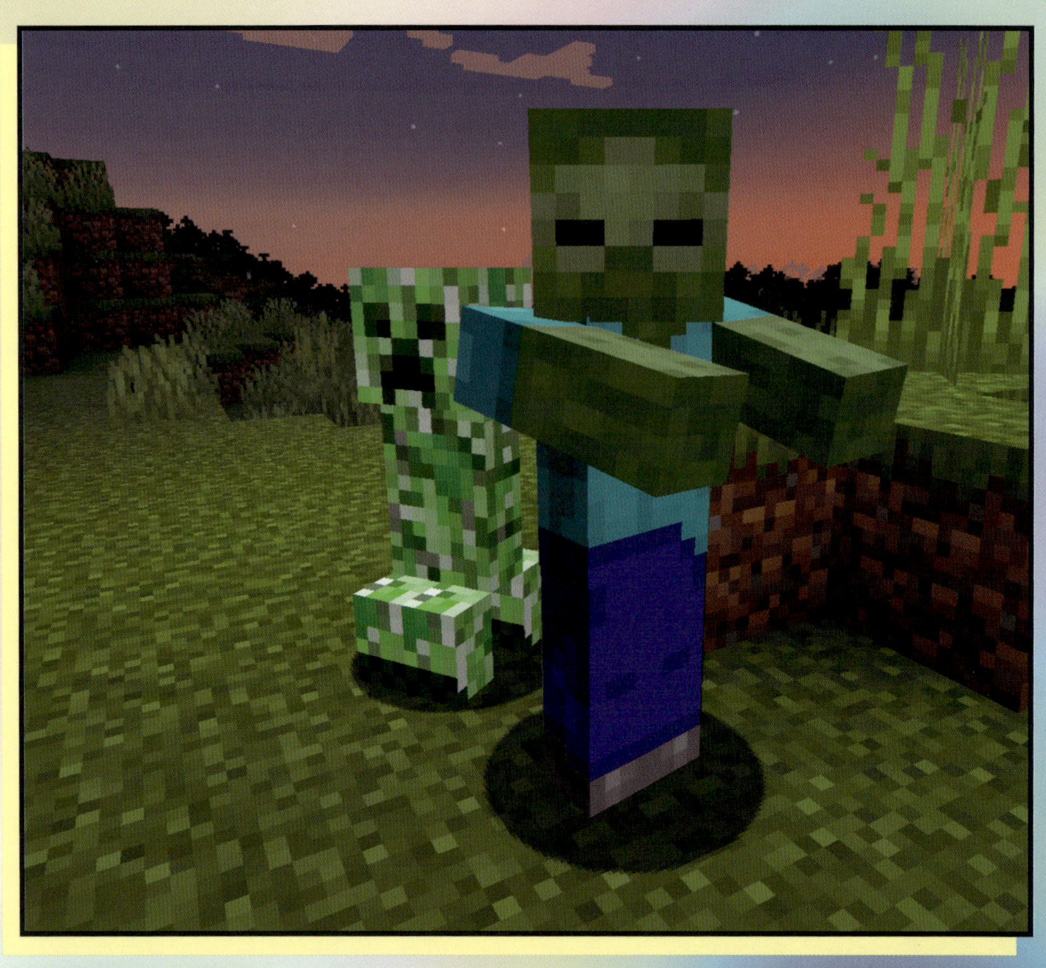

His early videos showed him playing games such as *Minecraft*.

He also made videos talking about other YouTube channels.

After a few years, Jimmy's channel became more popular.

In 2016, he quit college to focus on YouTube.

UP NEXT!

Going viral.

Rise to Fame

In 2017, MrBeast made a video of himself counting to one hundred thousand.

The video went viral. It gained six and a half million views in just a few days.

MrBeast hired four friends to help him run his channel.

He did impressive things such as leaving a $10,000 tip at a restaurant.

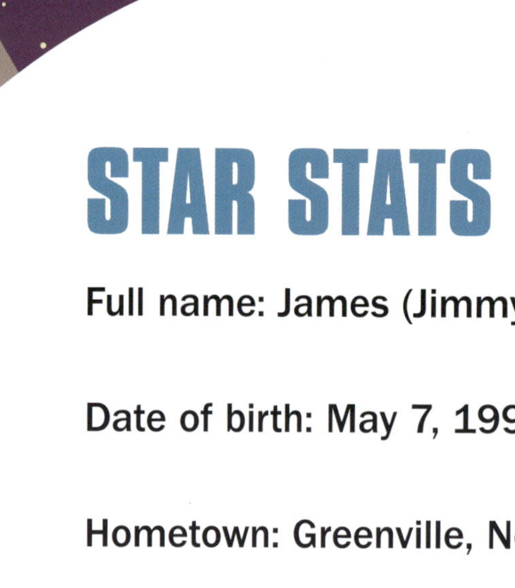

STAR STATS

Full name: James (Jimmy) Stephen Donaldson

Date of birth: May 7, 1998

Hometown: Greenville, North Carolina

HONORS

MrBeast won the Streamy Award for Creator of the Year four years in a row, from 2020 to 2023.

He was named one of *Time* magazine's 100 most influential people of 2023.

MrBeast became YouTube's most subscribed channel in June 2024.

He held competitions to win money and big prizes.

The more MrBeast gave away, the more views his channel got.

UP NEXT!

Using fame for good.

Giving Back

MrBeast wanted to use his fame to make the world a better place.

He raised millions of dollars to help the environment.

In 2020, he started a channel called Beast Philanthropy.

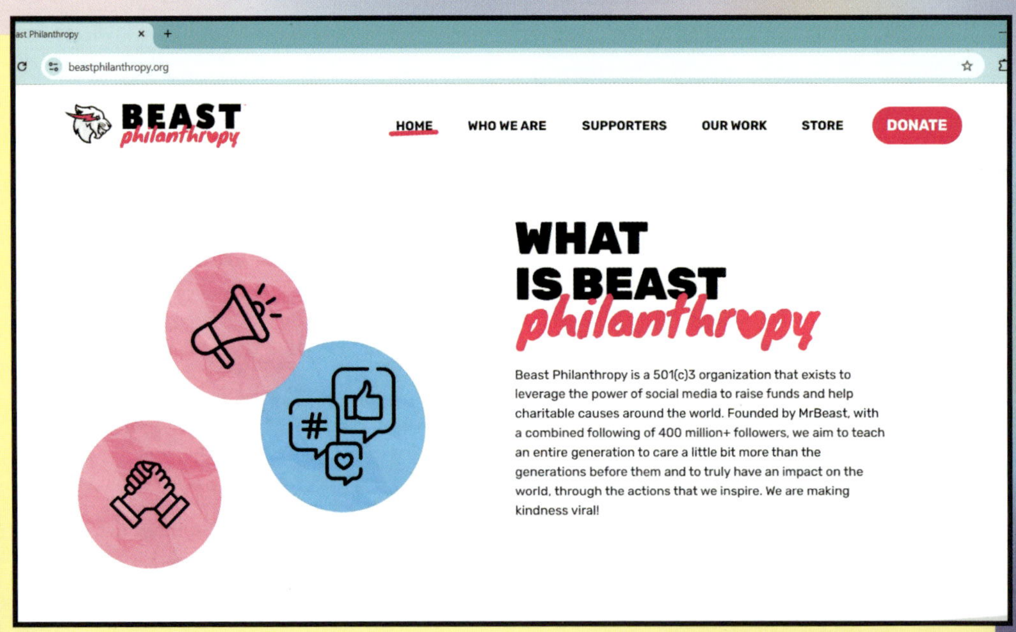

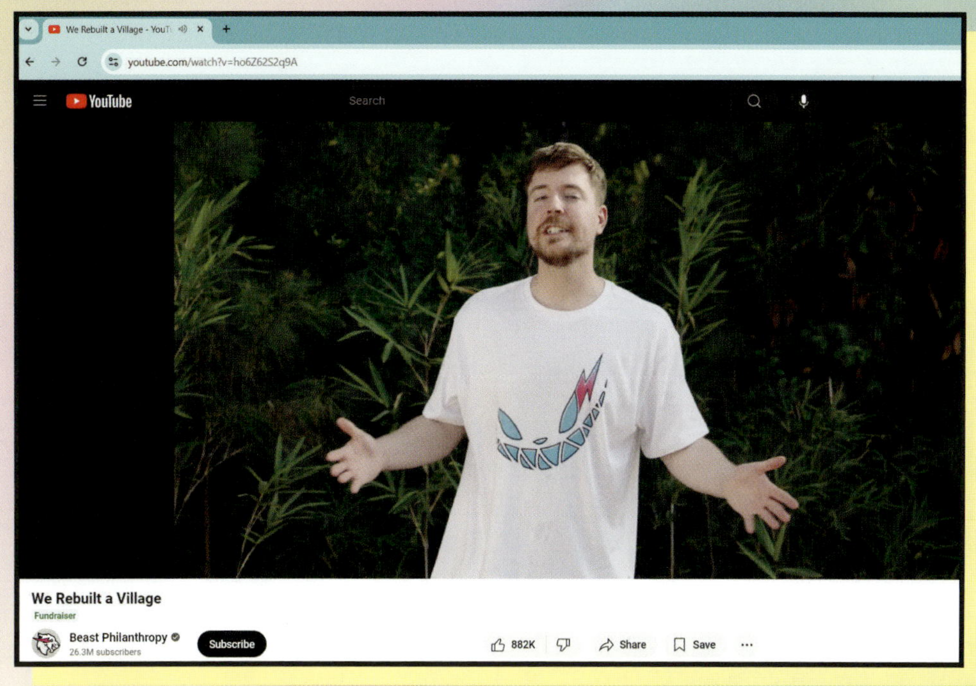

This channel helps provide food and housing to people in need.

MrBeast has many different YouTube channels.

He also owns a chocolate company and a burger company.

MrBeast employs more than 250 people.

His main channel has over 315 million subscribers. It continues to grow.

MrBeast has a lot of exciting plans for his channels and team.

Just like MrBeast

MrBeast inspires people to be kind and give back. What or who inspires you? How can you use your strengths for good?

GLOSSARY

competition: a contest

employ: to pay someone to work

influential: having the power to make a difference

inspire: to make others feel good or want to take action

philanthropy: actions that help people, such as giving money

subscriber: someone who follows something such as a YouTube channel

viral: quickly and widely spread on the internet

CHECK IT OUT!

Beast Philanthropy
https://www.beastphilanthropy.org/who-we-are

Britannica Kids: YouTube
https://kids.britannica.com/students/article/YouTube/570787

Chapman, Ty. *Top 10* Minecraft *Players: An Unofficial List*. Minneapolis: Lerner Publications, 2025.

Kiddle: MrBeast Facts for Kids
https://kids.kiddle.co/MrBeast

Koestler-Grack, Rachel A. *Curious About YouTube*. Mankato, MN: Amicus, 2024.

Saunders, Catherine. *The World of MrBeast: The Ultimate Unofficial Fan Guide*. New York: Wren & Rook, 2024.

INDEX

PHOTO ACKNOWLEDGMENTS

Image credits: Alberto E. Rodriguez/Getty Images, p. 4; Monica Schipper/Getty Images, p. 5; Chris Unger/Getty Images, p. 6; Denise Truscello/Getty Images, pp. 7, 15, 19, 24; *Minecraft* screenshot by Angel Kidd, p. 8; Vivien Killilea/Getty Images, p. 9; Dave Kotinsky/Getty Images, pp. 10–11, 14, 25, 28; MrBeast, I Counted to 100,000! via YouTube, p. 12; AJ_Watt/ Getty Images, p. 13; AP Photo/Sthanlee B. Mirador/Sipa USA, p. 16; MrBeast, Last To Leave Circle Wins $500,000 via YouTube, p. 18; Steve Granitz/Getty Images, p. 20; Noam Galai/ Getty Images, p. 21; beastphilanthropy.org screenshot, p. 22; Beast Philanthropy, We Rebuilt a Village via YouTube, p. 23; Don Arnold/Getty Images, p. 26; Brendon Thorne/Getty Images, p. 27; Dave Kotinsky, p. 28. Design elements: oxygen/Getty Images; Medesulda/Getty Images.

Cover image: AP Photo/Sthanlee B. Mirador/Sipa USA.